T0368788

SERIES 208

In this book we examine how trees work, explore how seasons can affect certain types of tree and look at a variety of amazing and unique trees from around the world.

LADYBIRD BOOKS

UK | USA | Canada | Ireland | Australia
India | New Zealand | South Africa

Ladybird Books is part of the Penguin Random House group of companies whose addresses can be found at global.penguinrandomhouse.com.

www.penguin.co.uk   www.puffin.co.uk   www.ladybird.co.uk

Penguin
Random House
UK

First published 2020
001

Printed in China

A CIP catalogue record for this book is available from the British Library

ISBN: 978–0–241–41721–8

All correspondence to:
Ladybird Books
Penguin Random House Children's
One Embassy Gardens, New Union Square
5 Nine Elms Lane, London SW8 5DA

Animal Habitats

9780241416860

Baby Animals

9780241416907

Insects and Minibeasts

9780241417034

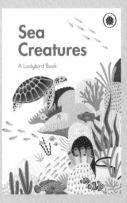

Sea Creatures

9780241417072

SERIES 208

Trees

A Ladybird Book

Written by Libby Walden
with botanical consultant, Dan Crowley

Illustrated by James Bywood

What is a tree?

Trees have existed for roughly 390 million years, and have grown on all seven continents (the conditions in Antarctica today mean that trees can no longer grow there). There are over 60,000 different species of tree, and around three trillion mature trees growing all over the world.

A tree is a woody plant that usually grows from a single, supportive stem known as a "trunk". Trees can grow to great heights and they are often topped with a crown made up of many branches and leaves. Beneath the trunk, usually below the surface of the soil, are the roots.

Like all plants, trees need sun, water and nutrients in order to grow. Different species have different needs — some like waterlogged soils while others prefer dry conditions — but, usually, three main parts of a tree are key to its survival:

- The roots anchor the tree in place and soak up the water and nutrients from the soil.

- The trunk keeps the tree stable and connects the roots to the crown. It transports water, sugars and nutrients between the two areas of the tree.

- The leaves in the crown help the tree to breathe. They contain chlorophyll, which gives leaves their green colour. Leaves turn light energy from the sun and carbon dioxide from the air into sugars to help it grow.

Crown

Leaf

Branch

Trunk

Root

Why are trees important?

Trees are amazing plants. They provide shade to humans and are living habitats to hundreds of species, including insects, fungi, birds, mammals, mosses and plants.
They can even benefit human health, as certain medicines are made using tree bark, oil or fruit – for example, aspirin (a painkiller) comes from the willow tree.

Trees also help to fight climate change by cleaning the air as they make their food. Air is made up of different gases, including oxygen (the gas that humans need to breathe to survive) and carbon dioxide. Carbon dioxide is mostly created by large vehicles like cars and planes, but too much of it in the air can contribute to global warming. Trees use carbon dioxide to make their food in the following way:

1. The tree roots soak up water from the soil.

2. The leaves take in carbon dioxide from the air and light from the sun.

3. The tree then uses light energy to turn carbon dioxide and water into oxygen and a natural sugar, called "glucose".

4. The tree stores and uses glucose as food.

5. It releases oxygen through its leaves, creating cleaner air for humans to breathe.

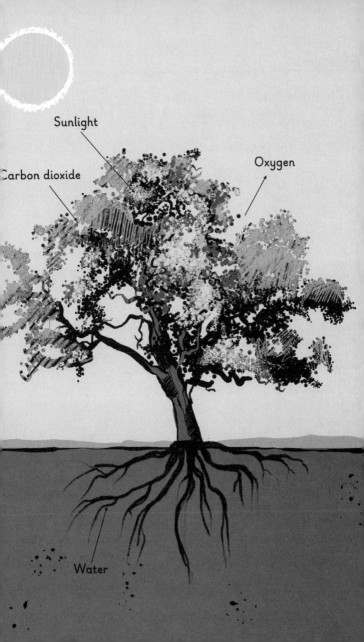

Sunlight

Carbon dioxide

Oxygen

Water

How a tree grows

A tree begins life as a seed, but not all seeds will grow into trees. Seeds need certain conditions to grow, including the right amount of air, water and light, as well as the correct temperature. These conditions all have to be just right to give the seed the best chance of growing into a tree.

Once a seed has settled in the earth, it uses stored energy to send out a root to search for water and nutrients. This root anchors the seed in place to give it stability as it grows.

The seed will then send out a shoot in search of sunlight. When the shoot pops out above the ground, the plant is known as a "seedling". As it grows, the seedling will use its leaves to start making its own food.

When it has grown to be around a metre (3 ft, 3 in.) tall, the young tree becomes a "sapling". Saplings often grow quickly and many species start to grow foliage at this stage.

Once the tree begins to produce flowers and fruit, it is described as a "mature" tree. This is often the longest phase of the tree's life and, depending on the species, a healthy tree can flower and produce fruit for hundreds of years.

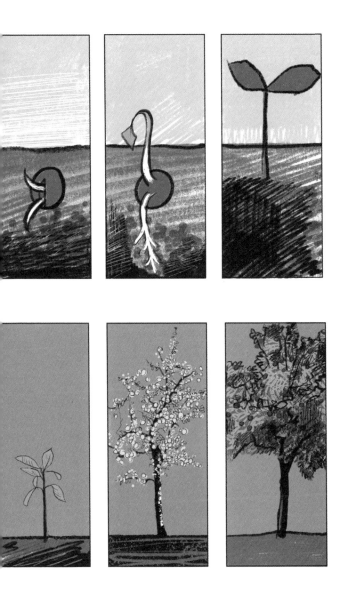

Tree fruit and seeds

At the right time of year, one of the easiest ways to identify a tree is to look at the fruit growing from its branches. Each species of tree produces a different type of seed case, which is called its "fruit".

Fruits grow in many different shapes, sizes and textures – from hard nuts to soft berries – and they can contain a single seed or have lots of seeds hidden inside.

How many of these tree fruits do you recognize, and do you know which tree they come from?

1. Acorn (common oak)
2. Samara (sugar maple)
3. Berry (red mangrove)
4. Capsule (horse chestnut tree)
5. Cone (Scots pine)
6. Catkin (silver birch)
7. Capsule (American sweetgum)
8. Pod (Judas tree)
9. Drupe (silver lime)
10. Aril (yew)

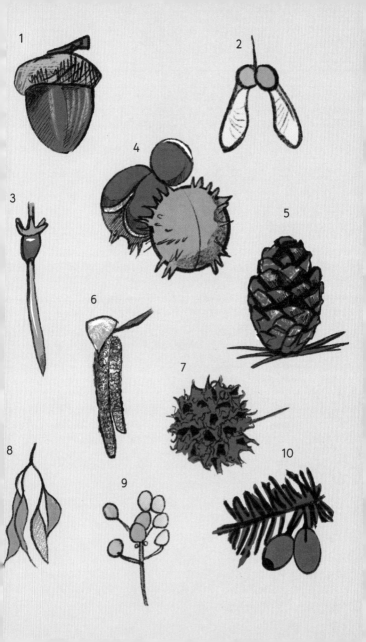

Inside the trunk

Hidden inside the thick, woody stem of most trees are five different layers that grow and change as the tree ages. Each layer within the trunk plays a very important role in keeping the tree healthy and strong:

- The outer bark is the protective, waterproof "skin" of the tree.

- The inner bark is made up of a special tissue called "phloem". This carries sugars from the leaves to the rest of the tree.

- The sapwood contains both living wood and a special tissue called "xylem". Xylem carries water and dissolved nutrients from the roots to the rest of the tree.

- The cambium is a thin layer of living cells that produces new layers of phloem and xylem every year. This is why tree trunks and branches get thicker as the tree gets older. It also causes ring-like patterns to appear inside the trunk as new sapwood is created. We are able to work out the age of most trees by counting the number of rings, or cycles of growth, hidden inside the trunk – one ring for every year of its life.

- The heartwood in the centre of the trunk is made up of non-living wood and can sometimes be a different shade to the rest of the trunk. This is because it contains decay-resisting chemicals.

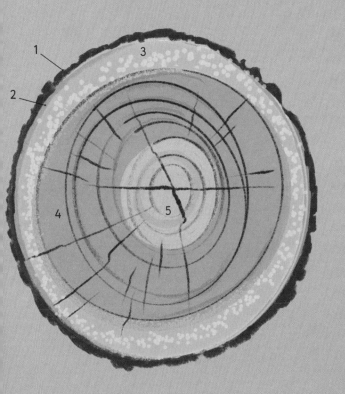

1. Outer bark
2. Inner bark
3. Cambium
4. Sapwood
5. Heartwood

Deciduous and evergreen

Trees can be divided into two main categories: deciduous and evergreen. In general, deciduous trees change colour and lose their leaves seasonally, while evergreens appear to stay green all year round.

As the days grow shorter in the autumn, the leaves of many deciduous trees change colour and break off from the branches. Woodlands and forests containing species of deciduous trees can turn the most amazing colours – from orange, brown and purple to red, gold and yellow.

In mild, or "temperate", climates deciduous trees "shut down" for the winter to save energy. The tree no longer needs its leaves to produce food, as it will survive the cold months on its food stores. As the leaves begin to wilt and fall, chlorophyll (the green dye in leaves) starts to break down, and other colours within the leaves are revealed.

In the spring, deciduous trees wait for the long days and warm temperatures to return before they start to grow new leaves again. They don't want to be tricked by short spells of warm weather, as cold can kill new leaves.

The thick leaves found on evergreen trees are suited to harsh, cold conditions. The tougher leathery leaves remain on the branches as they help to keep moisture in. This helps evergreen trees to stay healthy even when water or nutrients in the soil are difficult to find.

Common oak

The Białowieża Forest is one of the largest original lowland forests left in Europe. Stretching 1,192 square miles (3,086 square km) across Poland and Belarus, the forest is protected by its UNESCO World Heritage status. It is home to the world's last remaining European bison, as well as centuries-old common oak trees.

The common oak is a large, deciduous tree with rough bark and shallow-lobed leaves. Native to much of Europe, these trees can vary enormously in shape and size, as their growth depends on their growing conditions. Given enough space, the common oak will form a wide-reaching crown, supported by strong branches.

This tree species is also a habitat for lots of other plants and animals. Many animal and insect species are adapted to live in oak forests, particularly insects such as the stag beetle. Different mosses, lichens and fungi are also found growing on common oak trees.

Oaks tend to start producing their nuts, known as "acorns" or "oaknuts", when they are around 40 years old, and the most fruitful trees are often at least 100. In the past, people harvested acorns to create flour for breadmaking, but this doesn't happen anymore, leaving birds, squirrels and other woodland mammals to collect acorns in peace.

Coast redwood

Deep in the Californian Redwood National Park, soaring
high above the Douglas firs, western hemlocks and grand
firs, is Hyperion, the world's tallest known living tree.
This coast redwood stands at 115.6 metres (379 ft, 3 in.)
tall – that's 22 metres (72 ft, 2 in.) higher than New York's
Empire State Building, and 19 metres (62 ft, 4 in.) taller
than London's Elizabeth Tower (the home of Big Ben).

As an enormously tall species of tree and in order to survive,
the coast redwood needs to absorb as much water and
nutrients from the ground as it can. It has a large, shallow
root system that fans out from the trunk, reaching distances
of up to 30 metres (98 ft, 5 in.) away. Coast redwoods have
also been known to weave their roots between those of other
trees, which can help to keep the tall trees stable in wet and
windy weather.

The Pacific coast of North America is home to many other
huge conifers. As well as the tallest tree, the largest (by
volume) also grows there. It is a giant redwood known as
"General Sherman". The giant redwood and coast redwood
are closely related to each other and share other similarities
as well as size. For example, they both have very impressive
bark – not only can it grow up to 60 cm (24 in.) thick, but it
also contains protective chemicals to help guard the tree
against damage caused by wildfires.

Yoshino cherry

For two weeks of the year, thousands of people flock to the local parks and gardens of Japan to celebrate the springtime season of *sakura*, the blossoming of cherry trees. One of the most famous spots to celebrate is the Hirosaki Castle Park in Tokyo, home to over 2,500 cherry trees, including the most popular variety, the Yoshino cherry.

This cherry tree is particularly admired, as its almond-scented blooms change colour as they develop – from dark pink buds to light pink flowers that then fade to white. When it is young, its leaves are a near bronze colour, but they quickly turn dark green once the blossom is shed and small black cherries start to appear.

The Yoshino cherry tree is considered to be an ornamental tree. This means it is planted purely for the beauty it brings to outdoor spaces. Some ornamental trees, like the Yoshino cherry, do still produce fruit, but the produce often tastes too sour for humans to eat.

The ancient tradition of *hanami* – flower viewing – is very popular in Japan, although celebrations have spread into other Asian countries, Europe and the United States. People gather in huge numbers to picnic beneath the short-lived flowers and celebrate the beauty of nature and life itself.

"Gum trees"

Australia is home to over 800 species of eucalypts, otherwise known as "gum trees". They dominate parts of the Australian landscape to form forests and woodlands in almost all environments, except the areas of drier desert land.

The mountain ash is both the tallest species of eucalyptus – growing 70 to 110 metres (230 to 361 ft) – and the tallest hardwood tree. It grows in cool, mountainous regions and mild, or "temperate", rainforests, thriving in damp conditions. Young mountain ash trees are quick growers, with some shooting up to 2 metres (6 ft, 7 in.) every year.

The enormous Blue Tier Giant dominates the space in the Blue Tier Forest Reserve in Tasmania, Australia. It sits between the sassafras, myrtle beeches and celery-top pines, with a trunk that measures 19.4 metres (64 ft) around. It would take about fifteen people to wrap their arms all the way around it!

The foliage, white autumnal flowers and capsule fruit of the mountain ash's crown provide food for many different animal species, including endangered Leadbeater's possums, yellow-bellied gliders, koalas and wedge-tailed eagles. The hollow base of the Giant is large enough for a person to stand up in, and provides shelter for birds, possums, bats and insects.

Baobab

The baobab grows across the arid savannahs of Africa. It has green leaves and white flowers that open at night but smell rather unpleasant to humans. The flowers begin to open in the late afternoon, attracting bats and insects, but by the following dawn the flowers have withered and fallen.

It is a long-lived tree. Unlike other tree species, the baobab doesn't develop growth rings, but instead it hollows with time. This makes it a very difficult tree to age accurately but scientists are confident that one found specimen is over 1,200 years old!

The baobab has been nicknamed Africa's "Tree of Life", as it can survive in extremely dry conditions. It is able to store over 100,000 litres (21,997 gal.) of water in its trunk, which swells out to accommodate the water within. This gives the tree a bowed trunk and makes it look like it has a bloated stomach – a bit like a human's when they have eaten too much!

One of the biggest threats to the baobab is the African elephant. When water is scarce, elephants have learned to strip the soft bark and dig into the inner flesh of the tree to reach the water inside. The baobab is able to regenerate over time, but if elephants repeatedly visit the tree or damage it too badly, the tree will eventually dry up and die.

Silver birch

Like many other birch trees, the silver birch has a white bark, which makes it easier to spot among other trees. It has diamond-shaped leaves, with small teeth along their edges, and, as it gets older, the tree's bark forms rough ridges at the bottom and it loses its white colour.

The distinctive white bark of birches makes them a very popular garden species – some growers even polish the tree trunks to keep them as white and clean as possible! Some birches have bark that peels off in large, paper-like plates, which can be collected and used to start campfires.

The silver birch is often described as a "pioneer species", which means they are able to grow quickly in bare, open ground and help the soil by recycling nutrients. The widespread roots of the silver birch draw nutrients from soil further away to help the tree grow and develop.

In the autumn, when the birch sheds its leaves, these nutrients are recycled and returned to the earth beneath the tree. This improves the soil quality, helping other plants and trees to thrive, and attracts and provides food for many insect species.

Bald cypress

The bald cypress is a wetland tree that thrives in areas of calm, shallow water. Native to the United States, it is usually found in the warm, humid south-eastern states, although they can grow as far north as Indiana and Illinois.

Trees that grow in waterlogged or submerged soil often form large roots that appear to grow from the tree's trunk, above the base. These thick, sturdy roots are known as "buttress roots" and they are designed to help stabilize the tree in its wet habitat and in the loose soil.

When a bald cypress spends most of its time surrounded by water, it will grow distinctive roots that grow upwards, rather like the stalagmites found in caves. These roots have come to be known as "knees". The "knees" break the surface of the water and often grow up to 1 metre (3 ft, 3 in.) tall.

It has only recently been discovered that these unusual appendages have a particular purpose. They are breathing roots, designed to increase the oxygen supply to the tree's underwater root system.

Topiary

Topiary is the art of pruning and training trees or shrubs to grow in particular shapes, from pyramids and spheres to animals and faces. Records of topiary gardening date back to ancient Rome, when the Roman historian Pliny the Elder described the ornamental gardens of Caius Martius. He wrote that Martius used trees to create "living sculptures" of past battles and hunting scenes.

Eye-catching examples of topiary can be found in many places, from cottage gardens and local parks to the terraces of monarchs and emperors. Evergreen trees are often used in topiary, as they ensure that the design is on display all year round. Yew and box are particularly popular plants to use as they have thick, dense foliage, which is useful for creating solid-looking shapes.

The oldest topiary garden in the world can be found in Levens Hall, Cumbria, England. Originally created in 1694 by French gardener Guillaume Beaumont, there are over 100 sculptures in the gardens that still grow to Beaumont's original designs. To maintain the crisp edges of each shape, trained gardeners work for months on the sculptured trees and even use powered lifts to prune the highest parts of the trees.

Weeping willow

Usually found near bodies of water, the weeping willow is a graceful tree with drooping branches and long, slender leaves. Some people believe that it got its name because raindrops falling from the tips of the leaves make it look like the tree is crying. In Britain, the tree was so closely linked to crying and grief that in the nineteenth century, illustrations of weeping willows were used on gravestones.

Despite its mournful name, the weeping willow is actually a thriving habitat for wildlife. The bark is popular with wood-boring insects, such as carpenterworms and willow borer weevils. These then attract insect-eating birds, like the great spotted woodpecker. The light, slender twigs of the tree also make excellent nests for songbirds, such as the marsh wren or Baltimore oriole.

Willows produce a particular chemical in their bark and sap, called "salicylic acid". This chemical has been used by humans since the time of the ancient Greeks and Egyptians as a medicine for pain relief. In nature, white-tailed deer are often seen rubbing their antlers on the bark of the willow to relieve any itching caused by bone growth.

Horse chestnut

The horse chestnut tree is native to the Balkan forests of south-east Europe, but has grown outside of its natural range for hundreds of years. The tree is now more common outside of the Balkan area than it is within it and today, horse chestnut trees are actually at risk of extinction in the Balkans.

In late spring, the horse chestnut is covered in white flowers that appear in cone-shaped clusters, known as "candles". Within each flower, there is a spot of colour at the base of the petals, which can either be yellow or red.

These colours are very important to nectar-collecting creatures, such as bees. If the spot is yellow it shows that an insect has not yet visited the flower. If it is red, the nectar has already been collected. Insects recognize these colours and they will only visit flowers that are still yellow. During the summer, most of the flowers will develop into red-brown shiny seeds, surrounded by spiky green shells or husks.

In the UK, the horse chestnut seeds are used to play a game known as "conkers". Holes are drilled into the seeds so they can be attached to a piece of string. One player will hold their conker by the string, while the other player hits theirs against it. They then take it in turns until one conker cracks and breaks. The last standing conker is the winner!

Dragon blood tree

The distinctive dragon blood tree can only be found on the high mountain plateaus of Socotra Island in the Indian Ocean. Forming one of the oldest forest communities, these trees are well adapted to their dry, rocky environment.

Dragon blood trees have a very unusual umbrella-like crown, which shades the earth beneath the tree to help stop water evaporating from the soil near the roots. Their leaves are also all found on the top of the tree, to help maximize their access to sunlight and to any water vapour in the air.

But it is not the unusual shape of this tree that makes it so famous. If the bark is cut or tapped into, the tree will release a bright red resin that looks like blood. This is what gives the tree its common name. This resin is highly prized as a traditional medicine, but locals are only allowed to harvest the crimson resin twice a year, as the tree population has become scarce.

Dragon blood trees are vulnerable and the biggest threat they face is climate change. The species relies on certain weather patterns, particularly a regular monsoon season for water, but, due to the effects of global warming, the annual period of rain it needs is becoming less and less regular.

Tropical rainforests

Tropical rainforests are often considered to be centres of biodiversity – areas of land that contain a large variety of plant and animal life. The warm temperatures, long hours of sunlight and regular rainfall experienced within tropical rainforests create the ideal conditions for plant and tree species to thrive.

The largest tropical rainforest in the world is the Amazon of South America. It is twice the size of India and is believed that at least ten per cent of all known species on earth live here. Its tree population is estimated at numbers close to 400 billion across 16,000 different species, including the huasaí palm – which can reach heights of 20 metres (65 ft, 7 in.) – the rubber tree and the stilt-like walking palm.

Such a large variety of plant life creates competition between the plants as they fight each other for space, light, nutrients and water. Rainforests grow in layers, and the most successful tree species are the ones that grow quickly. The Brazil nut tree can reach heights of up to 50 metres (164 ft), growing quickly through the top of the rainforest canopy to make sure it has as much sunlight as possible.

Common holly

Native to Europe and western Asia, the holly tree likes moist, shaded conditions and is found in a variety of environments, from beech and oak forests to wild hedgerows. Mature trees can grow up to 25 metres (82 ft) and can have a trunk of up to 1 metre (3 ft, 3 in.) across.

Common holly leaves are often spiky, although on wild trees they become less spiky further up the tree. This is because the lower sharp-edged leaves are used to protect the base of the plant against the damage small ground animals could cause. However, common holly hedges or bushes that are found in gardens or parks often remain spiky all over, as the plant tries to defend itself against the "damage" caused by being cut or trimmed.

The bright red berries of the common holly may be poisonous to humans, but they are an important food source for birds in winter. The mistle thrush, in particular, is known to aggressively defend a holly tree against other birds, fighting off competition for its much-needed food supply.

In Celtic mythology, it is said that the holly tree controls the dark, winter months and symbolizes peace and goodwill. Its glossy evergreen leaves and bright red berries are strongly associated with winter festivities, as they add a burst of colour against ice and snow.

A Ladybird Book

collectable books for curious kids

What to Look For in Spring

9780241416181

What to Look For in Summer

9780241416204

What to Look For in Autumn

9780241416167

What to Look For in Winter

9780241416228

SERIES 205